EARTH SCIENCE—LANDFORMS Need to Know

SilverTip

Plateaus

by Ashley Kuehl

Consultant: Jordan Stoleru,
Science Educator

Minneapolis, Minnesota

Credits

Cover and title page, © simonkr/iStock; 3, © Ruslan Suseynov/Shutterstock, 5, © hadynyah/iStock; 7, © Celli07/iStock; 9T, © Ron and Patty Thomas/iStock; 9M, © anmbph/Shutterstock; 9B, © Different_Brian/iStock; 10, © Gchapel/Shutterstock; 11, © Mlenny/iStock; 12, © Peter Hermes Furian/Shutterstock; 13, © vagabond54/Shutterstock; 14–15, © Shensheng Zhou/Shutterstock; 16–17, © manavision/Shutterstock; 19, © Starcevic/iStock; 21, © Alexandree/Shutterstock; 22–23, © Josemaria Toscano/Shutterstock; 25, © Myroslava Bozhko/Shutterstock; 27, © klenger/Shutterstock.

Bearport Publishing Company Product Development Team

President: Jen Jenson; Director of Product Development: Spencer Brinker; Managing Editor: Allison Juda; Associate Editor: Naomi Reich; Associate Editor: Tiana Tran; Art Director: Colin O'Dea; Designer: Kim Jones; Designer: Kayla Eggert; Product Development Assistant: Owen Hamlin

Statement on Usage of Generative Artificial Intelligence

Bearport Publishing remains committed to publishing high-quality nonfiction books. Therefore, we restrict the use of generative AI to ensure accuracy of all text and visual components pertaining to a book's subject. See BearportPublishing.com for details.

Library of Congress Cataloging-in-Publication Data

Names: Kuehl, Ashley, 1977- author.
Title: Plateaus / by Ashley Kuehl.
Description: Minneapolis, Minnesota : Bearport Publishing Company, 2025. | Series: Earth science. Landforms : need to know | Includes bibliographical references and index.
Identifiers: LCCN 2024006095 (print) | LCCN 2024006096 (ebook) | ISBN 9798892320528 (library binding) | ISBN 9798892325264 (paperback) | ISBN 9798892321853 (ebook)
Subjects: LCSH: Plateaus–Juvenile literature.
Classification: LCC GB571 .K84 2025 (print) | LCC GB571 (ebook) | DDC 551.43/4–dc23/eng/20240215
LC record available at https://lccn.loc.gov/2024006095
LC ebook record available at https://lccn.loc.gov/2024006096

Copyright © 2025 Bearport Publishing Company. All rights reserved. No part of this publication may be reproduced in whole or in part, stored in any retrieval system, or transmitted in any form or by any means, electronic, mechanical, photocopying, recording, or otherwise, without written permission from the publisher. Bearport Publishing is a division of Chrysalis Education Group.

For more information, write to Bearport Publishing, 5357 Penn Avenue South, Minneapolis, MN 55419.

Contents

The Roof of the World 4
High and Flat 6
Alike and Different 8
Crash, Slide, and Crumple 12
Moving Magma 16
Carving Out New Landforms 20
Salty, Wet Plateaus 24
Minerals and Farms 26

Lava Makes Plateaus 28
SilverTips for Success 29
Glossary 30
Read More 31
Learn More Online 31
Index .32
About the Author 32

The Roof of the World

Just north of Asia's Himalaya Mountains, about four and a half million people live on the Roof of the World. They have made their home on the Tibetan Plateau (pla-TOH). This flat stretch of land sits higher up than many mountains. This is how it got its nickname.

The Tibetan Plateau is 14,800 feet (4,500 m) above **sea level**. It is the world's highest plateau. The plateau stretches across about 1 million square miles (2.5 million sq km). That makes it the largest plateau, too.

The Tibetan Plateau is called the Roof of the World.

High and Flat

About one-third of Earth's land is covered in plateaus. These landforms are flat areas. They sit higher than the land around them.

At least one side of a plateau has a big drop-off. The land directly next to it is much lower.

Plateau comes from an old French word meaning flat. Over time, the word took on another meaning. It can also mean something that doesn't change. These landforms are unchanging across large areas.

Alike and Different

Plateaus share some things in common with other landforms. Both mountains and plateaus rise high into the sky. However, mountains are pointy at the top. Plateaus are flat.

Plains are also flat. But unlike plateaus, plains aren't higher than the land around them.

Some plateaus are found alongside mountains. The Altiplano plateau, or Andean plateau, sits between two ranges of the Andes Mountains.

A mesa (MAY-suh) is even more like a plateau. This is a mountain with a mostly flat top and at least one **steep** side. However, a mesa has a smaller surface at the top than a plateau does.

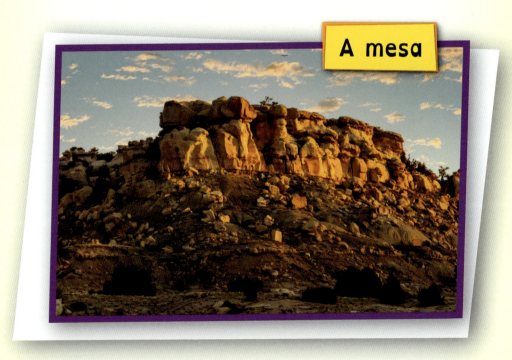

A mesa

A butte (BYOOT) is another landform with a flat top. All of its sides are steep. But a butte is even smaller than a mesa.

Crash, Slide, and Crumple

Plateaus stand tall, but they are caused by something deep underground. Earth's crust is made of many huge pieces of rock called **tectonic plates**. The plates are always slowly moving. As they do, plates may push into one another.

Tectonic plates fit together like the pieces of a puzzle. There is little space between them. The plates move very slowly. They go about 1 to 2 inches (3 to 5 cm) a year.

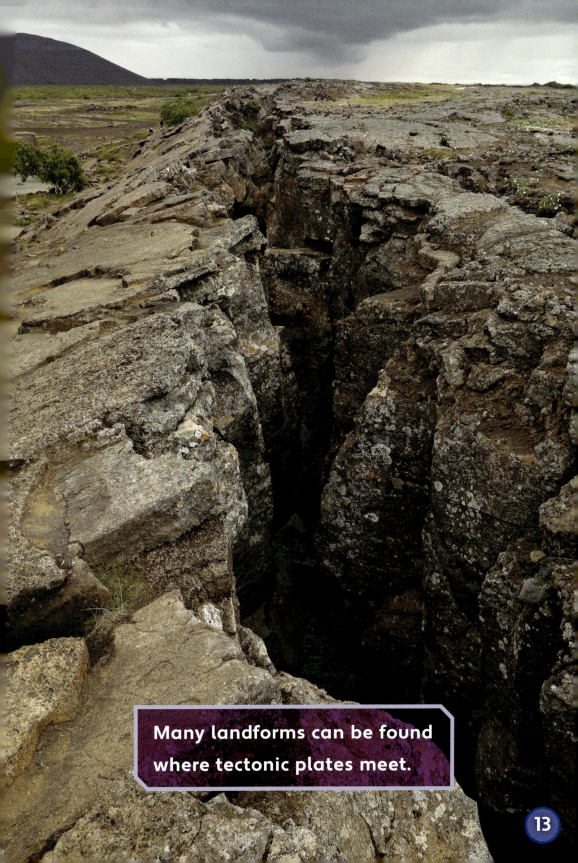

Many landforms can be found where tectonic plates meet.

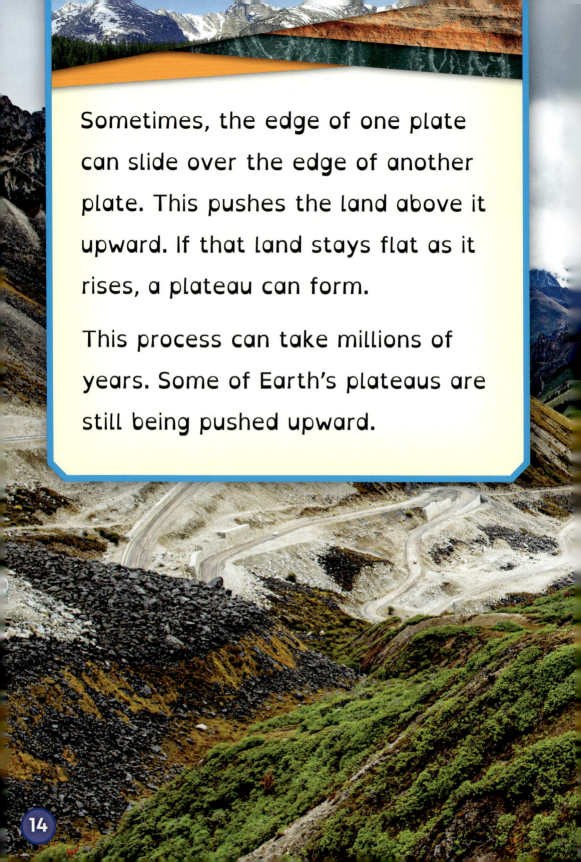

Sometimes, the edge of one plate can slide over the edge of another plate. This pushes the land above it upward. If that land stays flat as it rises, a plateau can form.

This process can take millions of years. Some of Earth's plateaus are still being pushed upward.

The tectonic movement that formed the Tibetan Plateau also formed the Himalayas. These plates are still moving. However, they are going more slowly than they did in the past.

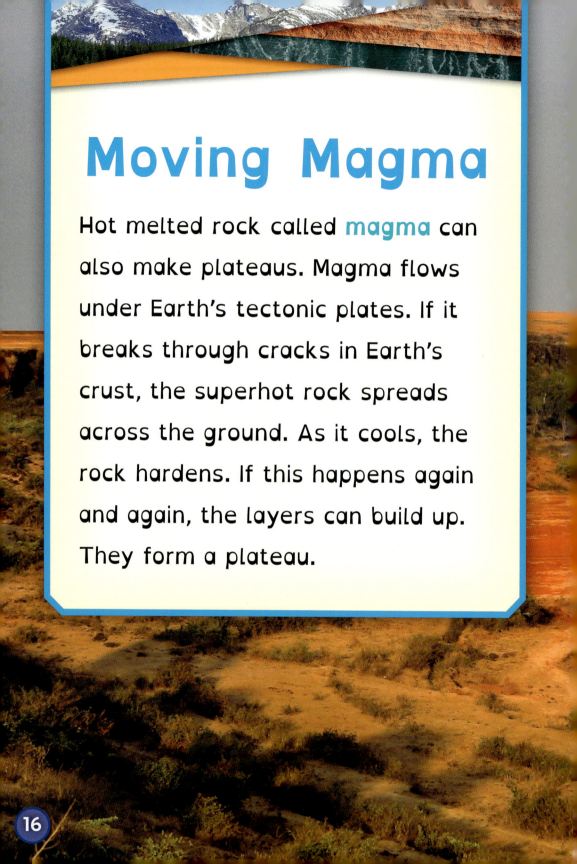

Moving Magma

Hot melted rock called magma can also make plateaus. Magma flows under Earth's tectonic plates. If it breaks through cracks in Earth's crust, the superhot rock spreads across the ground. As it cools, the rock hardens. If this happens again and again, the layers can build up. They form a plateau.

The hot melted rock is called magma when it is underground. But when it comes to Earth's surface, it is called lava. It breaks through at a spot called a volcano.

Sometimes, magma presses up but does not break through Earth's surface. Magma might push up the flat, rocky surface above it. This lifts the land up. As the hot magma hardens underground, the rock above it stays raised in the same shape.

Magma moving rock upward helped form the Colorado Plateau. This plateau covers about 130,000 sq. miles (337,000 sq km) of land. It touches parts of Arizona, Utah, Colorado, and New Mexico.

The Colorado Plateau

Carving Out New Landforms

It can take millions of years to form a plateau. Then, over time, the landform can change again.

Wind, water, and ice can break off tiny bits of a plateau. This is called **weathering**. Then, these pieces are washed away through **erosion**. What is left behind may no longer be a plateau.

Weathering can break off the sides of a plateau. They become less steep. The landform may turn into a mesa.

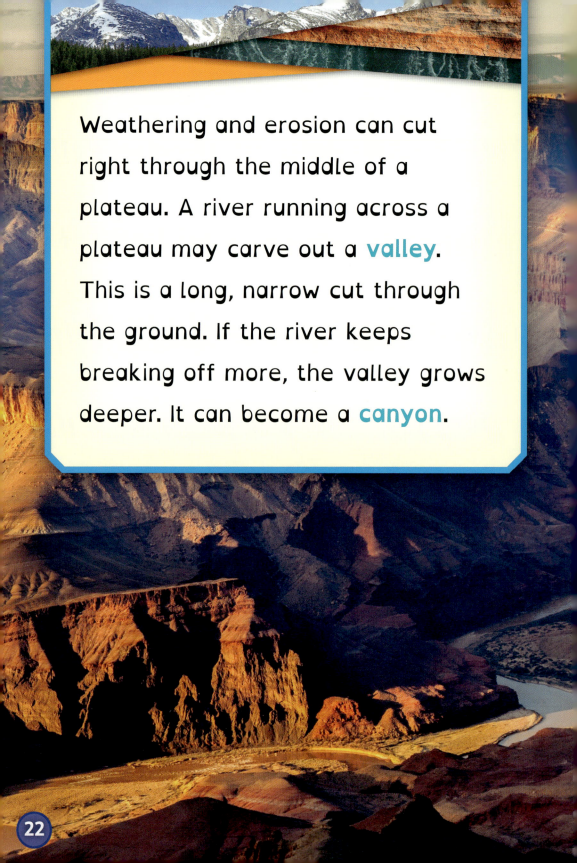

Weathering and erosion can cut right through the middle of a plateau. A river running across a plateau may carve out a **valley**. This is a long, narrow cut through the ground. If the river keeps breaking off more, the valley grows deeper. It can become a **canyon**.

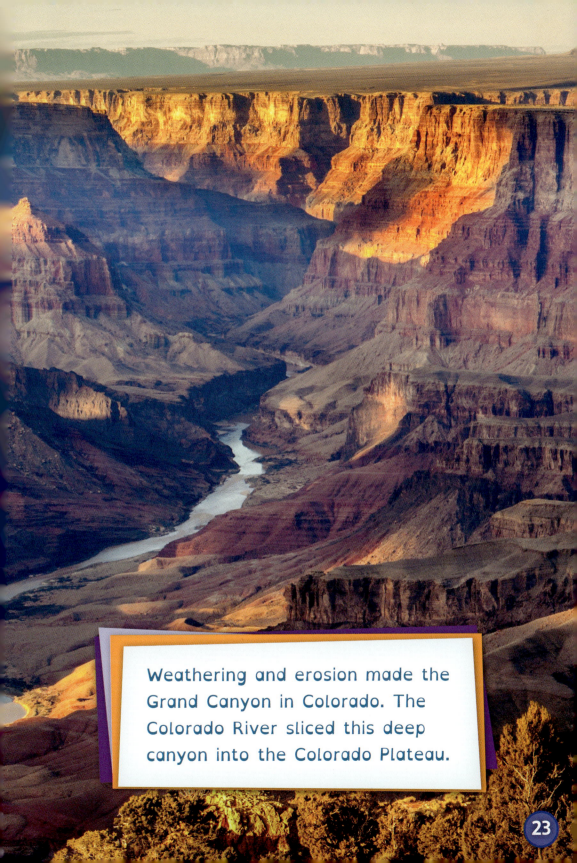

Weathering and erosion made the Grand Canyon in Colorado. The Colorado River sliced this deep canyon into the Colorado Plateau.

Salty, Wet Plateaus

The ocean floor has plateaus, too. Like plateaus on dry land, some ocean plateaus were formed by flowing magma. Others were made when tectonic plates moved.

Some ocean plateaus become islands. The plateaus are high enough to rise above the ocean's surface.

One plateau in the Indian Ocean can be seen from space! The Mascarene Plateau covers about 770 sq. miles (2,000 sq km).

Minerals and Farms

Plateaus shape not only the land but also life on Earth. People have long lived and worked on plateaus. We use the land to farm and raise animals. Some plateaus have **minerals** we need when making electronics or jewelry. Our relationship with these tall landforms will continue to change as they do.

> People get uranium from the Colorado Plateau. They use the mineral to make electricity. There is also baking powder and salt in the landform!

Lava Makes Plateaus

Some plateaus are made when layers of lava build up on Earth's surface.

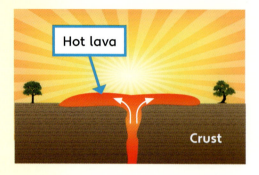

Lava flows to the surface from a crack in Earth's crust. As the lava cools, it hardens.

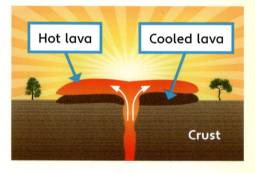

Later, more lava flows from the crack. It spreads over the same spot.

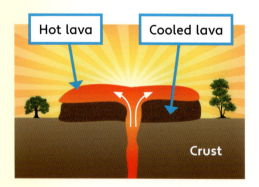

Lava keeps flowing to the surface, cooling, and hardening into stacked layers of rock.

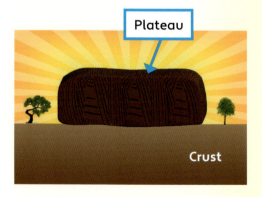

Over time, the layers build up into a plateau.

SilverTips for SUCCESS

★ SilverTips for REVIEW

Review what you've learned. Use the text to help you.

Define key terms

erosion
magma
mesa
tectonic plates
weathering

Check for understanding

How can magma and lava help make a plateau?

What can happen to Earth's surface when tectonic plates move?

Explain how weathering and erosion can change a plateau.

Think deeper

What kinds of landforms are in the area where you live? How does the land around you affect your life?

★ SilverTips on TEST-TAKING

- **Make a study plan.** Ask your teacher what the test is going to cover. Then, set aside time to study a little bit every day.

- **Read all the questions carefully.** Be sure you know what is being asked.

- **Skip any questions** you don't know how to answer right away. Mark them and come back later if you have time.

Glossary

canyon a deep, narrow valley carved out by a river

erosion the carrying away of rock and soil by natural forces, such as water and wind

landforms natural features on Earth's surface

magma hot melted rock found beneath Earth's surface

minerals solid substances found in nature that are not plants or animals

sea level the average height of the sea's surface

steep having a sharp slope or slant

tectonic plates huge pieces of rock that make up Earth's outer crust

valley an area of low land between mountains, hills, or parts of a plateau

weathering the breaking apart or wearing away of rock and soil by natural forces, such as water and wind

Read More

Bowman, Chris. *Zion National Park (U.S. National Parks).* Minneapolis: Bellwether Media, 2023.

Emminizer, Theresa. *Water and Rock: How the Grand Canyon Formed (Earth's History through Rocks).* New York: PowerKids Press, 2020.

Griffin, Annabel. *Core and Crust (One Planet).* Minneapolis: Hungry Tomato Ltd, 2021.

Learn More Online

1. Go to **www.factsurfer.com** or scan the QR code below.
2. Enter "**Plateaus**" into the search box.
3. Click on the cover of this book to see a list of websites.

Index

canyon 22–23

Colorado Plateau 18, 23, 26

Earth's crust 12, 16, 28

erosion 20, 22–23

farming 26

lava 17, 28

magma 16–18, 24

mesa 10–11, 20

minerals 26

mountains 4, 8–10

ocean plateaus 24

plains 8–9

river 22–23

tectonic plates 12, 14–16, 24

Tibetan Plateau 4–5, 15

valley 22

weathering 20, 22–23

About the Author

Ashley Kuehl is an editor and writer specializing in nonfiction for young people. She lives in Minneapolis, MN.